FAST AND SLOW ANIMALS

REPTILES

BY BRENNA MALONEY

Children's Press
An imprint of Scholastic Inc.

A special thank-you to the team at the Cincinnati Zoo
& Botanical Garden for their expert consultation.

Library of Congress Cataloging-in-Publication Data Available
Identifiers: LCCN 2022001821 (print)
ISBN 9781338836615 (library binding) | ISBN 9781338836622 (paperback)

10 9 8 7 6 5 4 3 2 1   23 24 25 26 27

Printed in China   62
First edition, 2023

Book design by Kay Petronio

Photos ©: cover top, back cover left, 1 top, 2 right: Heather Angel/Natural
Visions/Alamy Images; cover bottom, back cover right, 1 bottom, 2 left:
Tui De Roy/Minden Pictures; 4 top: Tui De Roy/Minden Pictures; 4 center:
Steven David Miller/NPL/Minden Pictures; 4 bottom left: H Schmidbauer/
Blickwinkel/age fotostock; 4 bottom right: Oliver Born/Biosphoto; 5 top:
Stephen Dalton/Minden Pictures; 5 center: Malcolm Schuyl/FLPA/Minden
Pictures; 6: Tui De Roy/Minden Pictures; 7: Tui De Roy/Minden Pictures;
8–9 all: Tui De Roy/Minden Pictures; 10–11: Erin Donalson/Getty Images;
12–13: Bence Mate/NPL/Minden Pictures; 14–15: Robert Valentic/NPL/
Minden Pictures; 20–21: James Gerholdt/Getty Images; 22–23: Olivier Born/
Biosphoto; 24–25: Michael Patrick O'Neill/Blue Planet Archive; 26: Auscape/
UIG/age fotostock; 27: CraigRJD/Getty Images; 28–29: Steven David Miller/
NPL/Minden Pictures; 28 tongue: Heather Angel/Natural Visions/Alamy
Images; 30 bottom left: Peter Finch/Getty Images; 30 bottom center: Nick
Garbutt/NPL/Minden Pictures. All other photos © Shutterstock.

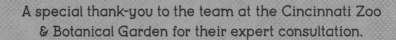

GALÁPAGOS
TORTOISE

PERENTIE

CONTENTS

MEET the REPTILES

Welcome to the world of reptiles! This group of animals includes lizards, snakes, turtles, alligators, and crocodiles. Reptiles have a lot in common. They breathe air. They don't have feathers or fur. They have **backbones**. They are **cold-blooded**. This means their body temperatures change with their surroundings.

How Reptiles Move

All reptiles can move!
But . . . how do they do
it? Some lizards crawl
on all fours. Others
run on their back legs.
Snakes slither on their
bellies. Turtles paddle
with their flippers.
Crocodiles waddle from
side to side. Reptiles
move in many ways!
Get ready to discover
how 10 reptiles can
travel, from the slowest
to the fastest!

5

#10 Slowest Reptile:
GALÁPAGOS TORTOISE

The Galápagos tortoise is the world's slowest reptile. It moves along at about 0.16 miles per hour (0.26 kph). To compare, a human walks at an average speed of 2.8 miles per hour (4.5 kph).

Why so slow? The Galápagos tortoise can't move much until its body is the right temperature. So it lies in the sun to warm up. Or it **wallows** in mud or soaks in water to cool down. It can spend up to 16 hours a day just resting! The rest of the day is spent eating grass, leaves, and cactus.

FACT

The Galápagos tortoise can live for more than 100 years.

GALÁPAGOS TORTOISE CLOSE-UP

A male Galápagos tortoise can weigh more than 500 pounds (226.8 kg). His shell can be 6 feet (1.8 m) long. He can be three times the size of a female tortoise.

SHELLS
Some Galápagos tortoises have saddleback shells. This one has a domed shell.

saddleback shell

SCALES
Thick, stumpy legs are covered with dry, hard scales.

SKIN
Most Galápagos tortoises have dull brown or gray skin.

PROTECTION
A Galápagos tortoise can withdraw its head, neck, and legs into its shell for protection.

TOOTHLESS
Galápagos tortoises don't have teeth! They grind up their food using the tough outer parts of their mouths.

SIDESTEPPING
A Galápagos tortoise doesn't move in a straight line. Its front feet are turned inward, so it moves slightly side to side when it walks.

FACT The Galápagos tortoise can only be found on the island chain of the Galápagos, off the coast of South America.

#9
GILA MONSTER

The Gila monster is one of only two **venomous** lizards in the world.

The Gila (HEE-luh) monster is the slowest lizard. It can reach a top speed of only 1.5 miles per hour (2.4 kph). This desert reptile is covered in bead-like scales. A Gila monster walks off the ground on short legs. It swings its tail from side to side for balance.

The Gila monster is named for the Gila River in Arizona.

The basilisk can be found in the rain forests of Central America.

#8 BASILISK

Most basilisks can run for about 15 feet (4.6 m) before they start to sink.

A basilisk can run faster than 7 miles per hour (11.3 kph). If chased by a **predator**, a basilisk can even sprint across water! How? This lizard has long back toes with **fringed** skin. When it smacks its feet hard on the water, the fringed skin unfolds. A pocket of air forms around its foot. As long as it moves quickly, the lizard can stay above the water.

#7
BEARDED DRAGON

When threatened, a bearded dragon can shift its body weight backward. That forces its body into an upright position so it can run on its two back legs. This position allows the dragon to change direction sharply. When a bearded dragon hits its top running speed, it runs at 9 miles per hour (14.5 kph).

A bearded dragon has a "beard" of spikes under its chin that can puff up depending on its mood.

FACT

Bearded dragons
come from Australia.

Black mambas live in Africa. They are one of the continent's most dangerous snakes.

The color in the black mamba's name refers to the inky-black color inside its mouth.

#6 BLACK MAMBA

A black mamba is a long and skinny snake. It can grow up to 14 feet (4.3 m) in length. Like many snakes, a black mamba moves in a sideways pattern. It looks like an S. Its scales grip the ground. It pushes off trees, rocks, and piles of dirt in its path. A black mamba can slither up to 12 miles per hour (19.3 kph).

#5

KOMODO DRAGON

The Komodo dragon is the world's heaviest and biggest lizard. It can grow up to 10 feet (3 m) long and weigh more than 150 pounds (68 kg). It may be big, but it isn't slow. The Komodo dragon can run up to 13 miles per hour (20.9 kph)

This powerful reptile has curved legs. It has a thick, muscular tail. It moves in a wavelike motion, swinging its head from side to side. It flicks out its long, forked tongue to taste the air and find food.

Komodo dragons are venomous and can kill **prey** quickly with a bite.

FACT

Komodo dragons live on only five islands in southeastern Indonesia, off the coast of Asia.

Racerunners can detach their tails if caught and will grow another one. **FACT**

SIX-LINED RACERUNNER

It is not hard to spot a six-lined racerunner. These lizards have six light yellow or white stripes down their backs. Catching a six-lined racerunner might be tougher. Racerunners are extremely fast. They zip along at 18 miles per hour (29 kph).

FACT Racerunners can be found in the United States and Mexico.

21

#3

NILE CROCODILE

A fast human can run 10–15 miles per hour (16.1–24.1 kph). The average Nile crocodile can reach speeds up to 22 miles per hour (35.4 kph). Worried? Don't be! Most Nile crocodiles don't run on land for more than a few body lengths. They use sneak attacks instead of chasing prey over long distances. This crocodile has three ways of moving. It can drag its belly and slide along while pushing with its feet. It can raise its body off the ground into a high walk. To gain speed, it can even **gallop**.

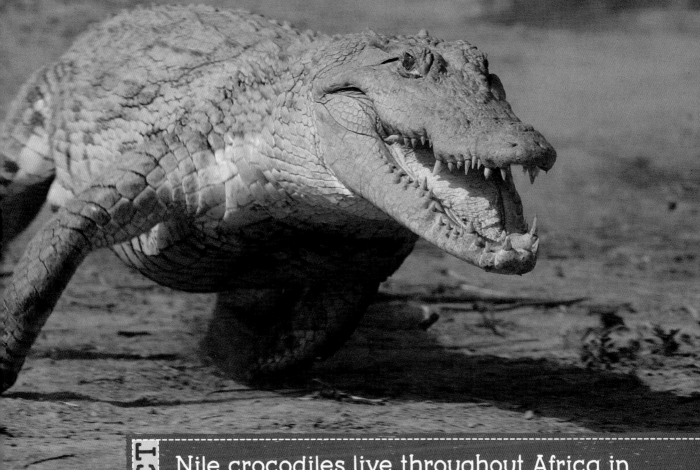

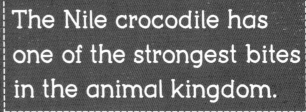

The Nile crocodile has one of the strongest bites in the animal kingdom.
FACT

FACT

Nile crocodiles live throughout Africa in rivers, freshwater marshes, and swamps.

Leatherbacks
cannot retract
their head or legs
into their shells like
other turtles can.

Leatherbacks are found in
oceans all around the world.

#2
LEATHERBACK SEA TURTLE

The leatherback sea turtle is the largest turtle. It can weigh up to 1,650 pounds (748.4 kg). It is a slow swimmer *most* of the time. But when it feels the need for speed, it can swim up to 22 miles per hour (35.4 kph).

This turtle is built for swimming. Its streamlined shell isn't hard like other turtle shells. It is thick and rubbery. Grooves on top of its shell allow it to cut through water easily. Long, strong front flippers paddle. Small back flippers help steer.

#1 Fastest Reptile:
PERENTIE

The perentie is the fastest reptile ever recorded. This slender lizard can reach speeds of up to 25 miles per hour (40.2 kph). For comparison, the top speed of the fastest man ever recorded is about 27 miles per hour (43.5 kph).

To reach great speeds, a perentie inflates and deflates the sides of its neck. This pumps a large amount of air into the lungs while the perentie is running. More air means greater speed for this lizard. It can run on all four legs or just its back legs.

FACT

Perenties can grow to be more than 8 feet (2.5 m) long.

SKIN SPOTS
Each perentie has unique spots, much like a human's fingerprints.

CURVED TEETH
Sharp, curved teeth tear apart food.

LONG NECK
A long neck inflates to bring more air to the lungs.

FORKED TONGUE
The perentie flicks its forked tongue to collect smells from the air to locate prey.

Perenties can be found in Australia.

FACT

LONG TAIL
A long, whip-like tail can be used for defense.

LEGS AND CLAWS
Powerful front legs and long claws help dig into sandy soil.

PERENTIE CLOSE-UP

The perentie may also stand upright on its back legs. It might do this to appear larger in size. It might also do this to get a better view of its surroundings.

REPTILES FAST AND SLOW

Now you know reptiles can move in many ways. They run. They slither. They crawl. They paddle. Some are slow, but many are not. The animals in this book are only a handful of the reptiles on Earth. There are more than 11,000 types of reptiles. Make it your mission to learn even more about how these amazing animals move and how fast they can go!

GLOSSARY

backbone (BAK-bohn) a set of connected bones that runs down the middle of the back; also called the spine

cold-blooded (KOHLD bluhd-id) having a body temperature that changes according to the temperature of the surroundings, like reptiles or fish

fringed (frinjd) something that resembles a border or edging

gallop (GAL-uhp) the way a horse or similar animal moves when it is running fast and all four of its feet leave the ground at the same time

herpetologist (hur-puh-TAH-luh-jist) a scientist who studies reptiles

predator (PRED-uh-tur) an animal that lives by hunting other animals for food

prey (pray) an animal that is hunted by another animal for food

scales (skaylz) thin, flat, overlapping pieces of hard skin that cover the body of a fish, snake, or other reptile

venomous (VEN-uhm-uhs) capable of putting poison or venom into another animal's body, usually by biting or stinging it

wallow (WAH-loh) to roll around in mud or water

INDEX

Page numbers in **bold** indicate images.

ABOUT THE AUTHOR

Brenna Maloney is the author of more than a dozen books. She lives and works in Washington, DC, with her husband and two sons. She is faster than a Galápagos tortoise but slower than a perentie, and she can't walk on water!